LEMON MERINGUE

100g (4oz) Butter

100g (4oz) Castor Sugar

3 Eggs seperated

Grated rind of one Lemon

2 Tbls. (30ml) Lemon Juice

200g (7oz) S.R. Flour

50g (2oz) Chopped Walnuts

125g (5oz) Icing Sugar

1. Preheat oven 170° Gas 3.
2. Line a baking ~~sheet~~ tin (11" × 7")
3. Cream butter & sugar, beat in egg yolks, rind, lemon juice & flour.
4. Press into tin, sprinkle walnuts
5. Whisk egg whites until stiff whisk in I/sugar 1tbls at a time.
6. Spoon meringue on top of walnuts
7. Bake for 35-40 minutes.
8. When cooled cut into 30 bars.

Why This Book?

This book is not like other cookbooks. It is not full of exotic, difficult recipes for people who spend long hours in the kitchen. It gives basic hints on how to make meals that are enjoyable, easy and healthy.

This book is about eating well on a limited budget and saving time. It's for people who like food but hate preparing it. It has short cuts for people who find work, children and other commitments mean that they have less time to prepare meals. It's also for people who want to use frozen, tinned and other convenience foods rather than long lists of raw ingredients because healthy eating does not have to mean cooking from scratch.

How to use this book

This book is based on the experiences of real people who have found ways of providing a healthy diet. It is intended to be used as a book you can dip into for ideas. A coding system is used so you can find bits that are most useful to you.

If there are particular foods you do not eat for any reason, perhaps on religious grounds or you are a vegetarian, or you just don't like them, then the hints and recipes can be easily adapted. Rather than give long lists of alternatives in the recipes, it is left up to you to decide what to change. Don't be put off if, for example, you only eat halal meat or you don't eat meat at all.

You will find symbols throughout the book. This is what they mean:

 lower cost

 more expensive

 little cooking

 no cooking

 saves time

 takes a little more time

 idea for one person

The idea of this book is to give you:

- ideas for healthy eating when money is limited

- quick, simple and inexpensive recipes for meals

- basic tips for beginners, as well as more advanced ideas

- tips on cooking for kids

- suggestions on cooking for small groups

- ideas to save time.

A Quick Guide

Healthy eating does not mean stopping eating what you have always eaten and changing to new, probably expensive, foods. It just means enjoying as wide a variety of foods as possible. If you remember to eat plenty of food rich in starch and fibre and not too much of the foods with fat, sugar and salt in them then you are eating healthily.

To try to get the right balance of foods, the guide below will help you to make sure you choose foods from each of the groups in the proportions suggested. All other foods and alcoholic drinks are 'extras' which are not essential and should be kept to a minimum.

Filler Foods

These should make up the main part of your meal and include: bread (all kinds), potatoes, rice, pasta, breakfast cereals. Wholegrain varieties contain more fibre and are more filling.

Fruit and Vegetables

These should be eaten at every meal and a good variety will give you most of the vitamins and minerals you need. Use any kind of fruit and vegetables, including fresh, frozen, tinned, dried and natural fruit juice.

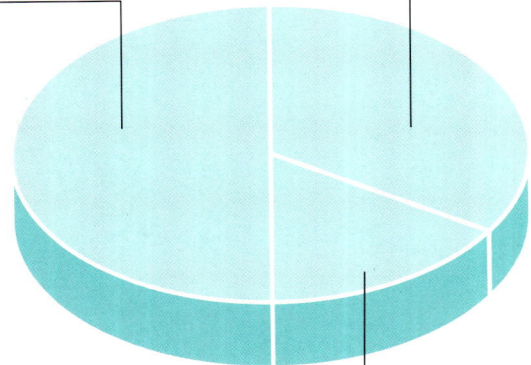

Protein

Include a little protein at every meal. Foods which contain protein include chicken, fish (including tinned), meat, eggs, milk, yoghurt, cheese, nuts, beans, lentils, peanut butter. Choose smaller portions of these foods and eat a variety for a good balance.

SHOPPING

£   lower cost

££   more expensive

little cooking

no cooking

saves time

takes a little more time

1   idea for one person

Ideas for keeping down food costs

Some general ideas tried by others:

£ 'I set aside the amount I can spend on food each week, that way I know what I'm spending.'

£ 'When I do take time to plan menus for a few days ahead, I know it saves me money as I buy foods less on impulse.'

££ 🕐 'I know I buy some ready made cakes, pastries, sauces, salads, and instant this or that. I know they cost more than the ingredients to make them but make sense when I'm in a hurry or if I'm eating by myself.'

£ 'I try to write down prices of basic foods and keep that list, so I know if they really are on special, but I sometimes forget to do it.'

Other shopping hints to try

£ Supermarket own brands are cheaper. They are often made by the same company as the 'advertised' brand.

£ If you have spare cash on a shopping trip, look for things reduced in price. It is worth buying things you use regularly while they are cheap.

Bread, cereals and potatoes

£ Bread may be sold for less when a supermarket is near to closing time. It can be a saving if you live near a supermarket or are passing by; but don't be tempted by other foods that can throw off your budget.

1 If you have a freezer buy small amounts of bread when reduced in price as above. If you slice it before freezing and put a few slices in a plastic bag in the freezer it can be quickly thawed and used. If you don't have storage space, buying bargains can be a waste.

£ Bread, rice, pasta, porridge, breakfast cereals, crackers and crisp bread are cheap sources of energy and are better for you than sugary foods. Eating wholemeal bread and bran cereals helps to prevent constipation.

(£)(1) To help spread costs buy cereal basics such as rice, pasta and porridge oats on different weeks.

(£) Some cereals which require more cooking cost less than ready-to-eat varieties. If you can't afford the time or if you don't like cooking, buy the easy to prepare varieties.

(£) Pound for pound potatoes are cheaper than ready made chips or crisps but they take time to prepare.

(1) Potatoes can usually be bought loose so smaller quantities can be bought. They store quite well if kept cool and in the dark.

Fruit

(£) Fruits or vegetables marked down in price can be a good buy if eaten right away. Bananas are often sold off by shops when skins start to darken. They are still good to eat.

(£)(1) Look out for offers of tinned fruit. Tinned fruit in juice rather than syrup is better for you, but compare prices. Fruit of any sort is good to include daily.

(£) Fruit drinks are less expensive than fruit juices but are not as good a buy unless they have added vitamins. Some drinks have no juice just flavourings and sugar.

(£)(1) You can buy fruit juice and add water and you will still get a good amount of vitamin C.

(£) Orange juice costs less than apple juice for the same quantity and has a similar vitamin content. If you can find concentrated apple juice it is cheaper. You add your own water rather than paying for it to be added and packaged in a vacuum pack.

Vegetables

(£) The lowest cost vegetables are usually cabbage, carrots, cauliflower and broccoli, mixed vegetables (frozen) and frozen peas.

(£)(1) When fresh vegetables are not in season, frozen or tinned ones will be cheaper and are just as good. They are also more convenient for one person.

(£) If vegetables are sold by the piece, choose the heaviest and largest. If sold by the pound (or kilogram), avoid ones with bulky leaves and stems that will be thrown away.

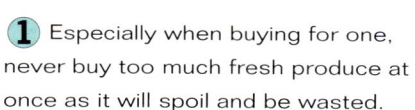

(1) Especially when buying for one, never buy too much fresh produce at once as it will spoil and be wasted.

(£)(1) Root vegetables such as potatoes, carrots, parsnips have little waste. To keep the goodness in, avoid peeling whenever possible.

(£)(1) Tinned tomatoes are a very good buy. They are useful to mash and use as a base on bread for a mini pizza or when mixed with other vegetables (leftover or not) or lentils to make a soup or spaghetti sauce.

Milk and milk products

Low-fat varieties of milk and cheese are healthier and not any more expensive. Semi-skimmed or skimmed is available fresh or as UHT.

(£)(1) UHT milk is handy to have on hand, costs less than fresh milk, can be stored in the cupboard until open and then should be stored as fresh milk.

(£)(1) Skimmed milk powder is the best buy in this group. Use it for making custard or if you do any baking. The powder keeps for a long time without refrigeration but once mixed up needs to be kept cool.

SHOPPING

(£) Milk tokens are available for children under five years of age whose parents are on income support and for pregnant women on income support. Children under two years of age should always be given whole milk.

(£)(1) A mild cheddar may be cheaper, but with a stronger cheddar you can use less to give more flavour. Scottish cheddar is a good buy, but watch for specials on other cheeses. Many supermarkets have cheese that is not pre-packed so you can buy the quantity you want. Most hard cheddars will keep well if kept cool and wrapped loosely. Some supermarkets have a variety of individual cheeses, they are fairly expensive, but can add variety if you are cooking for one.

Meat and alternatives

(£)(1) Baked beans are probably the best value for money around. Own brand are just as good nutritionally as others.

(£) Dried beans, peas and lentils (sometimes called pulses) are a good source of protein, vitamins, minerals and fibre. They are low in fat and cost a fraction of the price of meat. There are about 20 different varieties but many shops will sell a good pre-packaged range of 'own label' which are cheaper than branded goods.

(1)(⏱) Tinned beans and peas are also available and though more expensive pound for pound than the dried ones, they are easy to heat and add to other food.

(£)(1) Eggs are easy to cook and full of nourishment. But don't eat raw egg.

(£)(1) Get to know your local butcher. They can suggest the best buy for the week, suggest which cut to buy and how to cook it and weigh out small portions.

1 Buy sliced roast meat to enjoy a roast meal without buying a joint. Sometimes 'off cuts' of bacon are available.

1 Tinned stews and dried mince made from soya are usually cheaper than meat.

£ Mince is low in cost and has no waste from bone and gristle. Cheap mince is usually high in fat. It is better to buy a smaller quantity of leaner mince, so that you can eat all that you buy.

£1 Made up hamburgers are easy to use, but as they can be high in fat only eat them once a week at most.

£ Liver and kidney are very nutritious and quite cheap. If you are not sure about cooking them, check the recipe section for ideas.

Remember, liver should not be eaten during pregnancy.

£⏱ Fish is quick to prepare and particularly nutritious. Choose different varieties of fish as a change from meat. Mackerel, coley, herrings, fish fingers and tinned fish are good value for money.

Food labelling

Food labels are meant to give you information to help you choose between foods. Try to look at least for the following:

List of ingredients

This includes the food, additives and added water. They are listed in order of weight with the largest amount first but the actual weight is not listed. For example, with mushroom soup you get more mushrooms than other ingredients where mushrooms come near the top of the list. Most food additives have to be included on the ingredient list, either by name or E number. It also says what sort of additive it is, preservative, flavouring or colouring.

'Best before' and 'use by' dates

These are to help safeguard against food which may be unfit to eat or just unpleasant. 'Use by' is used for foods that can go off within a few days, such as meat pies or

chilled convenience meals. Eat it, cook it, or freeze it before that date or throw it out. 'Best before' is used for food that can be kept longer. When that date runs out, it doesn't mean that the food is necessarily dangerous but it may no longer be at its best. 'Use by' and 'best before' dates are based on the buyer following the storage instructions. If instructions are not followed, food will spoil more quickly and there may be a risk of food poisoning.

Measuring with no scales

The measures below use yoghurt pots, tablespoons and cupfuls. You can use them for other recipes you try. They are approximate but work pretty well.

Yoghurt pot measures - Imperial and Metric

Use any straight sided yoghurt pot marked 150g or 5.3 oz. Then reckon that one pot is approximately:

4oz/100g white flour
3oz/75g wholemeal flour
6oz/150g caster or granulated sugar
4oz/100g demerara or soft brown sugar
2oz/50g coarsely grated cheese (loosely packed)
$3\frac{1}{2}$oz/88g raisins
$2\frac{1}{2}$oz/63g chopped nuts
$2\frac{1}{2}$oz/63g desiccated coconut
$2\frac{1}{4}$oz/57g porridge oats
2oz/50g ground almonds
7oz/175g mincemeat
8oz/200g golden syrup
5 fluid oz/150ml liquid (eg water, milk)

Handy measures

Note that a tablespoon is bigger than a dessertspoon or a soup spoon. Approximate number of level tablespoons (tbsp) which correspond to 1oz/25g:

breadcrumbs, fresh	7
breadcrumbs, dried	6
packet crumbs	4
cheese (cheddar, grated)	3
cocoa powder	3
cornflour, custard powder, semolina	2
dried fruit (currants, raisins, sultanas)	2
flour, unsifted	3
rice, uncooked	2
rolled oats	4
lentils, split peas	2
suet (packet, shredded)	3
sugar, any kind	2
syrup, honey, treacle	1
margarine	1 inch cube

8 tablespoons liquid = 5 fluid oz = $\frac{1}{4}$ pint

You can also use a teacup to measure ingredients:
3oz dried pasta (enough for one person) = one generous cupful
2-3oz rice (for one person) = one cupful.

Kitchen safety

Make sure that curtains or blinds are well clear of the cooker, in case of fire.

Never leave hot oil (frying pan or chip pan) unattended on the cooker. Oil can overheat very quickly and catch fire.

If you do have a chip pan or oil fire: leave it where it is, turn off the heat, cover with a lid or damp cloth to smother the flame. DO NOT use water. Call the Fire Brigade if you cannot control the fire immediately.

Try to have a fire extinguisher or fire blanket in the kitchen.

If you have young children:
• make sure all dangerous substances are in a high cupboard, preferably locked
• make sure that electrical flexes do not overhang from any work surfaces or tables
• turn all pot handles to the side out of the reach of small children.

How to keep food fresh and safe

Most food hygiene is just common sense but the essentials are listed here as a reminder.

Wash your hands before and after touching food.

Don't leave food lying about uncovered in the kitchen.

If reheating food make sure it is hot right through. Lukewarm food, especially chicken and pork could give you food poisoning. Do not reheat food more than once. If you use a microwave remember to wait for standing time.

Once a can has been opened the contents should only be kept as long as fresh food. Do not leave food in the can, empty it into another container for storage.

Leftovers should be cooled as quickly as possible but wait until it is quite cool before putting it in the fridge.

preparing meat. It is important not to use a knife on uncooked meat and then use it for chopping something else.

Never keep cooked and uncooked meats on the same shelf in the fridge. Always keep uncooked

If you haven't got a fridge
- **eat meat and fish on the same day you buy them**
- **buy only small amounts of milk and keep as cool as possible**
- **cool any leftovers as quickly as you can and use the next day taking care to reheat thoroughly**
- **do not keep an open tin of a meat product overnight**
- **do not keep foods with cream in from one day to the next.**

If you use dried kidney beans, butter beans and soya beans they must be well boiled for at least ten minutes before completing cooking at a gentle simmer.

If flour has been sitting in a cupboard for a long time check best before date and also for weevils, which are small insects. If in doubt throw it out.

If you buy chilled or frozen foods, always take them home as quickly as possible.

Cover foods with wrapping or a plate when storing in the fridge.

Always wash your chopping board and knives before and after

meats as low down as possible and check that they don't drip onto other foods.

If you buy frozen chicken, defrost it safely (best in the fridge) until the ice crystals have melted. If you don't it may not cook right through and you can risk food poisoning.

To test that chicken is cooked, poke it with a fork or skewer. If the juices are clear it's cooked, pink juices mean it needs longer cooking.

Never refreeze food that has already been frozen.

BREAKFAST

£1 The easiest and most economical meal so try not to miss it.

If you are not a breakfast eater but get hungry mid morning then have a healthy snack ready such as bread and cheese and an apple, a fruit yoghurt or something easy, so you are not tempted by fatty, sugary snacks which could throw off your budget and your healthy eating plans.

No cook breakfasts

£1 Ready prepared cereals are convenient. Choose those without sugar coating.

£1 Muesli type cereal is more expensive but healthy. Choose one with no added sugar or honey. Soak overnight in milk and it's easier to eat.

£1 Porridge oats soaked the night before in milk or yoghurt need no cooking.

Prepared cereals don't need sugar added but if you are used to sweetness add some raisins, a banana or tinned fruit.

£1 Toast or bread with a thin spread of margarine or butter, peanut butter, or just jam or marmalade. Wholemeal bread is more filling; but any bread is better than a sugar coated doughnut or sweet biscuits.

A little cooking for breakfast

£1 Add hot water, milk or skimmed milk powder and water to a bowl of instant cereal for a quick hot breakfast.

£1 Scrambled or poached egg, a little bit of bacon and toast costs a few pence more and takes longer to prepare, but on a weekend two good meals may be enough for that day.

Fruit or fruit juice, milk or tea/coffee adds a good balance to any breakfast.

RECIPES

Method

1. Sprinkle porridge oats into salted water in a pan.
2. Bring to the boil stirring constantly.

Porridge
Serves One

½ pint / ¼ litre water

½ cup porridge oats

½ level teaspoon salt

(use about twice as much water as oats)

3. Simmer gently for about five minutes.
4. Add raisins if you like sweetness.

SNACKS

With different pressures on your life and foods available in many different situations, it is easy to find that you have been nibbling on snacks all day - grazing. It is still possible to eat a healthy diet without sitting down to a planned meal, but keep the following points in mind.

Keep a close eye on how much and what kinds of foods you are choosing. Some snack foods have a higher fat, sugar and salt content but they don't have to if you keep the food selection guide in the Healthy Eating section in mind.

Keeping track of where the money is going is more difficult if you are buying more snack type foods on a daily basis. You can keep healthy snack type items on hand at home.

It can be bad for teeth if you are eating sugar and sugary foods. The more often the food is in touch with teeth, the more chance there is of developing painful cavities.

Grazing for Health

If you are eating snacks out or at home, here are some healthy ideas.

Try to combine foods from the three food groups that are easy to pick up or have available.

Bread, rolls, pitta bread, chapati with fillings of:

- fish - tuna, sardines, pilchards
- eggs - egg salad or hard boiled eggs
- lean cold meats - slices, wedges or cubes
- cheese - all kinds, especially low-fat
- peanut butter
- banana
- vegetables - tomato, lettuce, cress.

Soups:
- add milk to tinned soups
- try split pea or lentil soup
- eat with bread, crispbread or crackers.

Baked potato with fillings:
- tuna mixed with green pepper, tomato and onion
- chopped bacon and pineapple

- tomato and sardine
- grated carrot and apple
- coleslaw
- sweetcorn, celery and ham
- smoked mackerel with orange segments.

Drinks:

- **choose fruit juice or milk**
- **avoid too many sugary drinks and/or tea or coffee with sugar**
- **if you choose a soft drink make it sugar free.**

Cereals: many breakfast cereals are healthy as a quick snack.

Fresh fruit, low-fat yoghurts, nuts and raisins:

- nuts are a quick, filling snack, but not for everyday as they are high in fat.

- raisins or other dried fruit like apricots and dried apple are an easy to eat snack, but not too often as they are sweet and sticky and therefore hard on teeth.

Scones and breads:

- plain scones, muffins or crumpets with a thin spread of jam
- also try fruit, currant, nut or seed bread.

LIGHT MEALS

Where to start?

Nothing beats bread as a basis for lunch. If buying for one choose small loaves or two or three brown, wholemeal, granary or white rolls to add variety.

Use the same basis as for main meals, starchy foods, vegetables and fruits and a bit of protein eg meat, fish, cheese etc to go with your

'I'm no good at packing a lunch to take with me; I know it's more expensive to buy a lunch, but what can I do?'
'Cheese toasties or just a cheese sandwich seems to be our standard lunch.'

bread. Choose milk, juice or water to drink.

Soup for lunch is a good way of including vegetables whether you make your own or buy tinned soup and add vegetables, beans or pasta to it.

Use salad from the previous day eg coleslaw, a mixed simple salad of chopped tomatoes or grated carrot to add to a roll for a packed lunch.

Many of the light meals ideas can be used as a main meal.

No cook meals

No need to make sandwiches, just toss a roll or two, a hard boiled egg and a yoghurt in a bag; and add an apple and milk in a flask. You could also use any leftovers from the evening meal that will carry eg a piece of pizza or quiche.

Using bread or rolls, add salad or leftover vegetable, coleslaw, tomato or grated carrot. Here are some ideas for other fillings:

- smoked mackerel mashed with yoghurt
- banana
- peanut butter
- scrambled egg
- cold ham or chicken
- tuna and sweetcorn
- sliced cheese and apple.

No time to prepare meals

If you are buying your lunch, bread or rolls are still your best basis. Two or three different kinds of rolls with a little margarine (if needed) plus a banana or some other fruit and a carton of milk is a filling low cost lunch.

Light meals at home

Wholemeal sandwiches or filled rolls, milk or fruit juice, yoghurt and fresh fruit are widely available. You pay someone else to put in the filling but this can make a quick and healthy snack lunch.

Pies, bridies or sausage rolls don't need to be given up altogether, but are very high in salt and fat so only eat them occasionally.

A canteen at work can be good value if you're living on your own but use the food groups in the food selection guide to help make your choices.

Soup and bread are a good standby.

Try baked beans, tinned fish, or cheese on toast and a simple salad or fruit with fruit juice or milk.

Baked potatoes with a filling are always a treat. They can be microwaved to save time and energy but boiled potatoes in their skins are a good alternative.

Two quick soups:

- a tinned soup made to go further by adding in leftover vegetables, cooked pasta, rice or potato
- already cooked vegetables, cooked rice or pasta, plus a stock cube and water makes an instant soup that gives better value in cost and nutrients than any bought instant soup.

RECIPES

Lentil soup
Serves One-Two

4 level tbsp lentils

half a carrot, 1 onion

1 medium potato

2 pints (1 litre) water

Method

1. Wash the lentils and drain. Chop or grate the vegetables.
2. Dissolve one or two stock cubes in two pints of boiling water in a saucepan.
3. Stir in lentils and other vegetables.
4. Cook for 20 - 30 minutes until lentils are very soft.
5. Add pepper and herbs if you have them. Serve with bread or crackers. If there is any left use the following day, add more vegetables, tomato or water and serve with rice and pasta.

Method

1. Melt margarine and stir in flour.
2. Add liquid gradually, stirring all the time.
3. Add tin of soup and stir until boiling.
4. Turn down heat and simmer for three minutes. Season if needed. Or add cooked pasta, rice or cooked pieces of potato as soup is heated.

Extended tinned soup
Serves Two

1 small tin soup

1oz (25g) 1 inch cube margarine

½ pint (¼ litre) stock, water, or milk and water mixed

1 tbsp flour

seasoning

Method

1. Lightly brown pitta bread under grill until softened and warm. Then cut in half and open to make a pocket. Leave to cool.
2. In a bowl, mix together cottage cheese, cheddar cheese, celery, spring onions, sweetcorn, salt and pepper.
3. Divide mixture between pitta pockets.

Pitta pockets
Serves Two

4oz (100g) cottage cheese

2oz (50g) cheddar cheese, grated

1 stick celery finely chopped

2 spring onions, sliced

half a 7oz (198g) tin sweetcorn and peppers

2 pitta bread

seasoning

Method

1. Mix all the ingredients together.
2. Lightly grease or add a small amount of oil to a frying pan.
3. Fry lightly, turning when lightly brown.
4. Serve with pickle or chutney and salad and brown bread.

Potato pancakes
Serves One - Two

1 - 2 medium raw potatoes, grated

1 egg

1 tbsp plain flour

seasoning

Any other starchy food can be used instead of potato eg carrots, turnip, swede, courgette.

Method

1. Put chopped celery and onion in a pan with the tinned tomatoes and cook gently until soft.
2. Blend soup and milk together then

Farmhouse tomato soup
Serves Two

1oz (25g) 1 inch cube margarine

1 onion

1 stick celery, finely chopped

8oz (225g) tin of tomatoes (chopped)

10oz (300g) tin condensed tomato soup

½ pint (250ml) milk

few drops Worcester sauce

2oz (50g) sweetcorn

seasoning

add to softened vegetables in the pan.

3. Add Worcester sauce (if you have it), sweetcorn and seasoning then bring to the boil and simmer for ten minutes.

Method

1. Mix apple, cheese, ham, peaches, nuts, and sultanas in a bowl.
2. Add yoghurt and seasonings and mix well.
3. Serve with crusty bread.

Winter salad
Serves Two - Three

1 red apple, chopped

2oz (50g) cheddar cheese cut into small cubes

2oz (50g) (1 or 2 slices) cooked ham cut into small squares

half a small tin peaches, drained and chopped

1oz (25g) about 2 tbsp peanuts

1oz (25g) 2 tbsp sultanas

half a 5oz (125g) carton natural yoghurt

seasoning

You can use the leftover peaches, juice and yoghurt to mix with some oatmeal, muesli or biscuit crumbs, as a sweet.

Method

1. Place lentils in water and stir until boiling.
2. Simmer gently until lentils are

Tomato and lentil soup
Serves One

1 tin tomato soup (medium size)

4 level tbsp lentils

1 pint (½ litre) water

pinch of basil (if you have it)

soft (about 20 minutes).

3. Add tin of tomato soup and the basil, reheat. Serve at once.

'I've always made liver and onions, I never realised it was healthy. Gives you the confidence to have a go.'

'As a student cooking on my own, I make a pot of a sort of vegetable sauce. I cook lentils as a base. Check at the greengrocers for what's on special and add these with tomatoes and herbs. I can stir it into rice, put on top of spaghetti or have it with potato and that's three easy meals with little preparation.'

Where to start?

Plan meals around the three food groups in the Healthy Eating section. Make the largest part of your meal bread, cereal (pasta or rice, or other grains) or potatoes. Add plenty of vegetables, fresh, frozen or tinned.

Then add a little protein from foods such as chicken, fish, eggs, milk, yoghurt, cheese, nuts, beans, lentils; whatever you can afford or have on hand. That means you are planning your meal around the starchy foods which are filling, give you fibre and are inexpensive and easy to prepare.

If you wish you can round off the meal with fruit or a pudding combining fruit, cereal, milk and yoghurt.

No cook main meals

Below are more specific ideas from the food groups that can be used for no cook main meals, followed by suggestions for putting them together as a meal.

Bread, cereals, potatoes:
- bread and rolls - choose from granary, wholemeal, French stick or pitta
- try instant mashed potato.

Vegetables:
- choose from fresh carrots, tomato, broccoli, cauliflower, cabbage, cucumber, green or red peppers, lettuce, other greens (use these uncooked)
- use tinned and preserved vegetables: try beetroot, pickles, sweetcorn, tinned carrots or green beans or mixed vegetables
- mix as a salad with a little lemon juice, herbs or salad cream.

Fruits:
- any fresh fruit in season
- tinned fruit
- fruit pie occasionally.

Meat and alternatives:
- try baked beans and other tinned beans eg kidney beans or chickpeas
- mix beans with other vegetables eg onion, cucumber or sweetcorn
- mash beans with tomato sauce and herbs for a tasty sandwich spread
- tinned fish can be bought with different flavoured sauces eg tuna, mackerel, sardines
- use cold cooked lean meats, eg liver sausage, ham, turkey, beef.

Milk and milk products:
- try different varieties of cheese and cottage cheese including low fat types
- choose low fat milks or yoghurts
- add milk to an instant custard or pudding
- try plain ice cream as a sweet.

Some menu ideas - no cooking
- **Tuna on wholemeal bread or toast**
- **Cold sweetcorn**
- **Plain yoghurt and sliced peaches.**

- **Grated cheese, grated cabbage and apple in pitta bread**
- **Carrot sticks**
- **Ice cream.**

- **Instant potatoes, sliced turkey and baked beans**
- **Beetroot**
- **Fresh fruit, cheese and crackers.**

Ready prepared meals or almost ready prepared meals

With prepared foods check the length of the ingredients list, sometimes the additive list is longer than the food list.

Keep in mind the same planning principles: starch, vegetables, some meat or alternatives. Choosing a pasta, rice, bread or potato dish is a good choice eg pizza, lasagne, cannelloni or fish cakes or shepherd's pie. Fish fingers are good value, grill them if you can.

££ These will always cost more because someone is doing it for you, but they are a way to get variety when cooking for one.

£ Baked potatoes are always a main or light meal treat. They cost less to prepare if you have a suitable microwave. If using a conventional oven a metal skewer put through them will reduce cooking time but do not do this with the microwave. Cook more than one to add to a soup or bake other food at the same time eg sausages or a crumble.

1 Salads also come ready to eat and give you variety when you're on your own. Choose one that's not loaded with dressing.

1 A fruit pie or crumble is a nice treat once in a while.

££ Fresh made pasta, ready to bake pizza bases or bread are available in most large supermarkets. Ready made sauces to add to them are also available, and are convenient for those who don't like preparation. If you can, have extra bread and a simple salad.

£1 Packet soups can be used in small quantities for soup or as sauces for savoury dishes. The packets can be resealed after use and keep for about three weeks.

Some menu ideas - a little cooking

- **Spaghetti and lentils with mixed vegetables, or add the lentils to a bought ready made sauce**
- **Grated cabbage and carrot with a little mayonnaise**
- **Sliced apples and pears.**
- **Boiled potatoes in their skins, mince and tomatoes**
- **Sweetcorn and peas**
- **Orange slices with custard.**
- **French stick, chopped tomato, grated cheese, cooked under the grill**
- **Cauliflower**
- **Stewed apple with pancakes.**

RECIPES

Method

1. Wash and scrape or peel carrot. Slice into thin coins or diagonal slices.
2. Cut the green pepper into thin slices and slice the onion and mushrooms thinly.
3. Heat the oil in small frying pan or wok over moderate heat for about two minutes.
4. Reduce the heat to low, add the vegetables, and stir constantly for one minute.
5. Add the hot water, stir the mixture and cover the pan tightly. Let the vegetables steam in the moisture over low heat for three or four minutes, or until they are tender but still crisp. Serve immediately with cooked rice or any pasta or potato.

Stir-fry vegetables
Serves One

3-4 mushrooms

quarter of a small green pepper

½ tbsp oil

1 small onion peeled

1 tbsp water

seasoning

This can be prepared in a wok, an electric frying pan or pot or an ordinary frying pan covered with a lid.

Method

1. Wash the rice thoroughly, then put in a saucepan with the water and salt if used.
2. Bring to the boil, turn down heat, then cover the pan and cook slowly for 10 - 15 minutes.

Plain white rice
Serves Two

8 level tablespoons long grain white rice

½ level tsp salt (leave this out if you are adding other foods)

½ pint (250 ml) water

Allow 2oz (four level tablespoons) of rice per person. Cooking extra means you can use it for a salad or reheat with vegetables.

Don't lift the lid or stir during cooking as the starch comes out and the rice clogs together. Keep the lid on until ready to serve, then stir gently with a fork.

White rice is polished so the goodness of the germ and bran is lost. Brown rice is more chewy in texture with a nutty flavour and is a valuable source of fibre and B vitamins. Brown rice uses the same method as white but can take 30 - 40 minutes to cook.

Method

1. Fry chopped onion until soft but not very brown.
2. Add curry powder and continue to fry for another two minutes.
3. Add chopped potato and fry for another five minutes.

Chicken and vegetable curry
Serves Two

1 medium onion (chopped)

1lb (550g) medium potatoes, chopped into small cubes

8oz (225g) tin of tomatoes

4oz (100g) 4 - 5 tbsp peas

4oz (100g) any other vegetable

8oz (225g) cooked chicken

$1\frac{1}{2}$ cups of water

$\frac{1}{2}$ tbsp oil

$1\frac{1}{2}$ tsp curry powder (add according to taste)

4. Add all the other ingredients except the water. Continue to cook until potatoes are done, adding water if the curry dries out.
5. Serve with rice and chapati.

Method

1. Cook the pasta according to the instructions on the packet.
2. Drain the brine from the tuna.
3. Lightly fry the onion in the oil until soft.

Tuna and pasta
Serves Two

1 medium onion, chopped

2 tsp vegetable oil

1 garlic clove, crushed (optional)

8oz (225g) tin tomatoes

7oz (200g) tin of tuna in brine

4oz (100g) $1\frac{1}{2}$ cupfuls pasta

2oz (50g) 3 - 4 tbsp frozen or tinned peas

2oz (50g) 3 - 4 tbsp sweetcorn

$\frac{1}{2}$ teaspoon dried basil (if you have it)

4. Add garlic, tomatoes, sweetcorn and basil. Mix well.
5. Add the tuna and mix well together.
6. Heat through and mix with pasta.

Method

1. Put flour, baking powder and bicarbonate of soda into a bowl. Mix to a smooth dough with the milk and the yoghurt.
2. Knead lightly until smooth.
3. Pat or roll out into a circle about eight inches (20cm) across.
4. Heat the oil in your frying pan. Add the circle of dough and fry for three minutes quite gently. Turn it over and fry the other side.
5. Preheat grill on medium.
6. Roughly chop the tomatoes and spread over the dough almost to the edge.
7. Place ham or vegetables evenly over the tomatoes and sprinkle on grated cheese and mixed herbs.
8. Place pan under the preheated grill for three or four minutes until the cheese is bubbly and turning to a golden brown.

If baking don't fry the base. Instead have oven heated to 220°C/400°F/ gas mark 6. Add toppings and bake for 15 - 20 minutes.

Pan-fried pizza
Serves Two

4oz (100g) 1 heaped yoghurt pot wholemeal plain flour or 1 pot half wholemeal, half white flour

$\frac{1}{2}$ tsp baking powder

$\frac{1}{2}$ tsp bicarbonate of soda

3 tbsp plain natural yoghurt

3 tbsp milk

1 tbsp oil

8oz (225g) tin tomatoes, drained

4oz (2 good slices) lean cooked ham chopped into squares, or mixed vegetables if you want a meat-free dish

large pinch mixed dried herbs (if you have it)

3 tbsp cheese, grated

(You can also do this in the oven which reduces the fat used.)

Method

1. Make diagonal slits down each side of the fish (not too deep).
2. Rub in black pepper and thyme.
3. Grill fish under moderate to high heat for ten minutes each side.
4. Serve immediately with boiled potatoes and a salad.

Grilled mackerel
Serves Two

1 cleaned (gutted) fresh mackerel

thyme (if you have it)

black pepper

Method

1. Poach the fish in the milk.
2. Melt the margarine in a pan and stir in the flour.
3. Add the milk from the fish to the flour and margarine paste stirring all the time.

Fish pie
Serves Three - Four

1lb (450g) coley or haddock

¾ pint (375ml) semi-skimmed milk

1oz (25g) 1 inch cube margarine

1oz (25g) 3 tbsp flour

black pepper

fresh parsley (if you have it)

mashed potato (for the top of the pie)

4. Add pepper and parsley to the sauce.

5. Flake the fish into a medium size

pie dish and pour on the sauce you have made.

6. Cover with mashed potato and bake in a preheated oven at 185°C / 370°F/gas mark 5 for 25 minutes.
7. Serve with peas.

Method

1. Cook the rice in boiling salted water until just going soft. Drain.
2. Fry the chopped onion, mushrooms, green pepper and garlic in the margarine until starting to go soft.

Tasty risotto
Serves Two

5oz (125g) 1½ cups long grain rice

8oz (225g) tin of tomatoes

¼ lb bag frozen peas

4oz (100g) mushrooms

1 medium onion

1 small green pepper

1 small can of kidney beans (or any other sort not in sauce), drained

1oz (25g) 1 inch cube margarine

pinch black pepper

pinch dried mixed herbs

3. Add the pepper, mixed herbs, tinned beans and tinned tomatoes with their juice to the vegetables and heat gently.
4. Stir in the cooked rice and frozen peas. Cook for ten minutes.
5. Serve with bread.

Method

1. Slice liver thinly. Use the best quality you can afford - it is still cheaper than most other meats. Pigs and lambs liver have a milder taste than ox liver.

2. Coat the slices in flour and a little seasoning.

3. Fry the slices in the oil or margarine for no more than five minutes, turning them once so they are brown on both sides.

4. Slice and fry the onions.

5. Add the onions to the liver.

Liver and onion casserole
Serves Four

1 tbsp oil or 1 inch cube margarine

3/4 lb (340g) liver

1lb (450g) onions

a little flour

seasoning

Method

1. Make the crumble by rubbing in the margarine into the flour ands oats.

2. Stir in the sugar and oil.

3. Grease a baking dish or loaf pan with a little fat.

4. Place the apples, dates, water and sugar in the dish.

5. Sprinkle the crumble mixture over the fruit.

6. Bake for 25 - 30 minutes in a preheated oven at 190°C/ 375°F/gas mark 5 until top is golden brown.

Apple and date crumble
Serves Two (or one serving hot, then one serving cold the following day)

Crumble:

3/4 oz (20g) a small cube margarine

1oz (25g) 3 tbsp wholemeal flour

1oz (25g) 4 tbsp porridge oats

1/2 oz (15g) 1 tbsp sugar

1 tsp oil

Filling:

One cooking apple, cored and chopped or sliced (no need to peel - just wash)

a few chopped dates, raisins, sultanas or other dried fruit

sugar to sweeten (optional)

KIDS

'But they like chips and burgers!'

'5 pm - what's for tea, mum? And I haven't a clue.'

Children over one year old do not need separate meals cooked for them. Any of the recipes in the other sections can be tried with children. Anything with pasta is popular eg tuna and pasta, macaroni cheese. Pizza is popular - try letting the kids put their own topping on.

Catering for Kids

Kinds of food

Help children get the right balance by choosing foods from the food groups from the guide in the Healthy Eating section. Young children enjoy food prepared simply. They usually like one food on its own and may be suspicious of sauces or spices that are new to them. Letting children help in food selection, preparation and serving may help to get them interested. Children are great imitators and will watch what foods you eat and drink.

Appetite

Your child's appetite can change from day to day. Some days they will eat non-stop, some days very little.

Dealing with not eating
Try to be relaxed at meal times. Avoid any suggestion of forcing, punishing or bribing kids to eat, even though it has been stressful to try to get the food on the table. Make eating a pleasant time for both you and your child.

Also their growth rate will change from year to year and thus their appetite changes.

What about snacks?

Young children have small stomachs and may not be able to eat much at one sitting, therefore they need between meal snacks. But sugary foods and drinks, or fatty snacks and sweets, will spoil their appetite for the next meal. These also do not have the nutrients your child needs and the sugary ones cause tooth decay. Nuts should not be given to small children because of the risk of choking.

Can I use convenience food?

Parents of young children often need ideas for food to prepare quickly. Milk, bread, cheese, eggs, raw fruit and vegetables are the original convenience food. Other suggestions for quick, economical, healthy and delicious meals:

- add milk instead of water to packet soup
- offer baked beans on toast
- try grilled fish fingers
- stir vegetables or pasta into a cheese sauce
- add milk or grated cheese to instant mashed potato
- add chopped fruit to instant custard or rice pudding
- stir a little muesli (or plain oatmeal) and fruit into yoghurt.

Are additives harmful to children?

Many foods need additives to keep them fresh and in good condition. However a small number of children are allergic to some additives, usually colourings. These are found in brightly coloured processed foods, so these can often be avoided by eating unprocessed food such as fruit, vegetables, cereals, milk, eggs, fish, and meat.

Healthier snack ideas:

- **bananas, pears, apples, satsumas**
- **dried fruits such as raisins, apricots or apple rings**
- **milk**
- **pure fruit juice diluted with water**
- **wholemeal, rye, oat or rice crackers**
- **wholemeal biscuits**
- **cereal with or without milk**
- **raw vegetables**
- **sandwiches, rolls or pitta filled with peanut butter, cottage cheese or fromage frais, mashed or sliced bananas, cheese or sardines and any salad foods.**

What about milk?

Ask your health visitor for advice about your child, but the following is a rough guide:

Under one year: breast milk or formula milk

One - Two years: use whole milk or silver top

Two - Five years: you can use semi-skimmed if you wish, provided your child is eating a well balanced diet.

RECIPES

Method

1. Sieve the flour and salt (or sugar if using) into a bowl.
2. Make a well in the centre and crack in the egg and add milk, a little at a time.
3. Stir well until you have a good pouring consistency.

Pancakes
Serves One - Two

4oz (100g) 1 yoghurt pot flour, wholemeal, plain or a mixture

$1/4$ level tsp salt

1 egg

$1/2$ pint (250ml) semi-skimmed milk

(If making sweet pancakes add 1 tbsp sugar instead of the salt.)

4. Lightly grease a frying pan.
5. Pour about quarter of a cup of the batter into the heated frying pan and swirl round.
6. Let the batter just cook until little bubbles appear and it starts to curl at the edges. Cook only slightly on the other side.
7. Keep warm and add filling when ready to serve.

Easy savoury fillings - grated cheese, cottage cheese, grated carrot, peanut butter. Ideas for sweet fillings - grated apple, sliced banana.

Method

1. In a bowl blend all of the cornflour with a little of the milk until you have a smooth paste.
2. In a saucepan heat the rest of the milk to boiling point (but don't let it boil hard).

Easy white sauce
Serves Two

1 level tbsp cornflour

$1/2$ pint (250ml) skimmed or semi-skimmed milk

seasoning

(Children will often eat things they might have rejected if it is served with a little cheese sauce, or curry, egg or tuna sauce. No recipe section is complete without this basic sauce.)

3. Gradually stir the milk into the cornflour mixture.
4. Pour the mixture back into the saucepan and heat gently, stirring all the time until it thickens. Season to taste.

Variations: cheese sauce - remove from the heat and add a pinch of mustard powder and 2 tbsp grated cheese; egg sauce - add 1 chopped hard boiled egg after removing from the heat.

Fruit lollies
· · · · · · · · · · · · · · ·

If you have a freezer you can freeze ice cube trays of fresh juice and use as a snack or at the end of a meal. Or mix plain natural yoghurt with fresh fruit and freeze.

GROUPS

££ **If you decide to get a take away meal you can make a great vegetable salad when ingredients are shared or finish with a fruit salad when everyone brings one fruit.**

£① Joining your cooking skills and meal ideas with others in a flat or people with similar ideas is a good alternative to eating on your own. Some people use a kitty and take turns in shopping, or each can bring an ingredient to a meal. It needs a little planning but in the long run saves money, time, and is fun and helps pick up new ideas.

Another idea is to focus on one nutritious, cheap but interesting dish eg bread, soup, pasta and add a dish or two to complement it. Let people help themselves so they can choose what and how much they like. It can save on preparation too and any leftovers can be shared.

Ideas for shared meals

The following are only suggestions. Only use one idea and make it a one course meal. Again the nutrition principles are the same, start with the starchy food.

Bread meal

Basics: loaves of fresh bread unsliced, two or three different kinds if you can afford them.

Variations: margarine, cheese, peanut butter, cottage cheese, tuna, a favourite spread, lettuce, tomatoes, onion, pickles, other raw vegetables in season.

 Everyone puts together their own meal and leftovers are reusable.

Soup meal

Basics (1): thick soup using lentils or beans, home-made or tinned, add in some pasta or rice.

Variations: raw vegetables, bread or rolls and fruit.

 Soup can be made in advance and reheated. Give it a try even if you're not a cook or get a friend to help.

Basics (2): pot of plain stock made from a stock cube.

Variations: bowls of hot rice, hot

noodles, chopped cooked meat, chopped spring onions, chopped cabbage or other greens, chilli or hot peppers, or other flavours you have on hand eg soy, Worcestershire, or brown sauce.

 Everyone fill bowls with foods they want , then ladles

harc-boiled eggs, chickpeas or kidney beans; thin pieces of cooked meat, cheese, onions or raw vegetables; peanuts or croutons (toasted bread cut in cubes); mayonnaise and another dressing or just oil and vinegar with bread or some crackers.

the hot stock over it. This may be a chance to try brown rice or a different type of pasta.

Rice meal

Basics: steamed or fried rice.
Variations: meat and vegetables stir-fried, curry, dhal or hot chilli beans (these can be bought in or ready to heat foods can be used); raw chopped vegetables, tomatoes, salad greens, hard boiled eggs, peanuts, raisins, chutney, or soy sauce.

 Eat lots of rice, a little meat and stretch out the meat with vegetables.

Salad meal

Basics: a big bowl of salad greens.
Variations: a small bowl of chopped

This is a good meal for summer when vegetables are cheaper and in season. Everyone could bring a different vegetable. This could be made ahead, but keep chilled.

Pizza meal

Basics: buy ready to cook bases, wholemeal if you can, and use a home made sauce of chopped tomato and tomato puree.
Variations: onion, mushroom, cheese, red or green peppers, sweetcorn, tuna, tinned pineapple cubes (in juice), herbs and spices.

Everyone can bring something different to put on the pizza. Leftovers can be eaten as a snack the next day.

RECIPES

Method

1. Heat oil or fat in large frying pan or saucepan.
2. Lightly fry onions, green pepper, garlic and lean mince until lightly browned, stirring frequently. If meat is fatty, let cool and drain off some of fat.
3. Add beans, tomatoes and chilli powder and mix well.
4. Simmer (turn down to let bubble gently) for half an hour, stirring occasionally. If mixture thickens add the water. Taste before serving and add more chilli if desired.
5. Serve with rice (use brown or long grain rice following package directions - allow 2 - 3oz per person), or serve with different types of bread.

Chilli con carne
Serves Eight

2oz (50g) oil or margarine

½ green pepper, chopped

1 medium onion, chopped

1 clove garlic or pinch garlic powder

1lb (500g) lean mince

2 x 14oz (400g) tins kidney beans

4 x 8oz (225g) tins tomatoes, chopped

1 - 2 tsp chilli powder (add more if you like it hot)

half a cup of water (add other vegetables to the chilli if you have them on hand)

seasoning

Method

1. Preheat oven to 220°C / 425°F/gas mark 7.
2. Scrub and prick two or three times with a fork.
3. Place on a tray in preheated oven (if no tray, just place on centre rack in oven).
4. Bake until tender when gently pressed (time will vary from about one to one and a half hours depending on size).
5. Remove from oven and cut a large cross on top of potato.
6. Squeeze gently to enlarge cut.

Baked jacket potatoes
Allow one large potato per person

7. Serve hot with one of the fillings suggested below (or make two or three if cooking for several people).

Ideas for fillings:

- cottage cheese and peach or pineapple
- grated cheddar cheese and chopped tomato/ham/onion
- coleslaw
- chilli.

Microwave Method

1. Prick the potatoes with a fork then place on kitchen paper in the microwave oven.

2. Cook on high, turning them over halfway through cooking until soft when gently squeezed. One potato will take 4 - 6 minutes, two will take 6 - 8 minutes, and four will need 10 or 12 minutes.

Method

1. Bring lentils to the boil in saucepan (watch for boiling over) and simmer for 20 minutes. Use cooked lentils in one of the two dishes below.

Basic cooked lentils
Serves Four - Six

8oz (200g) 16 tbsp lentils

1 pint (500ml) water

1 stock cube (any flavour)

1 bayleaf (or any herbs you have)

(Green, or continental, lentils give a good flavour.)

Method

1. Gently fry together oil or margarine, onion and garlic.

2. Add curry powder. Fry briefly.

Curried lentils
Serves Four

25g (1oz) 1 inch cube margarine

1 large onion, chopped

1 clove garlic, crushed

1 tbsp curry powder

1 tbsp lemon juice

herbs (if you have any)

3. Add to basic cooked lentils with 1 tbsp lemon juice and chopped parsley if available (or fresh coriander even better).

Method

1. Gently fry the onion and celery in the margarine.
2. Add the tin of tomatoes, oregano and garlic and meat.
3. Add the basic cooked lentils, carrot and potato.

Easy lentil stew
Serves Four

1oz (25g) 1 inch cube margarine

½ lb (250g) diced ham, or cooked mince

8oz (225g) tin tomatoes

½ tsp oregano

1 onion, chopped

2 stalks celery

1 grated carrot or courgette

1 large potato cut into small cubes

1 clove garlic, chopped

4. Simmer until the potatoes are cooked.
5. Serve with rice or bread.

Method

1. Heat the oven to 200°C / 400°F/ gas mark 6.
2. Wash and core the apples. Slit the apple skins around the middle.
3. Place the apples in a baking tin or oven proof dish. Put a tablespoon of

Baked apples
Allow one apple per person

1 cooking apple

1oz raisins

1 dessertspoon of clear honey

water per apple into the dish, this will stop the apples sticking or getting too dry.

4. Fill the empty core of each apple with raisins and top off with the honey. Bake in the oven for 20 - 30 minutes.

The apples are ready when they are soft. This can be tested by inserting the blade of a knife into the split skin.

5. Serve with natural yoghurt or fromage frais (if you have it).